DID GOD MAKE YOU HIS NEXT
CONSTRUCTION SITE?

Is there a mansion inside of me?

Third Edition

Graphics/ Cover designed by
IWRITEANDDESIGN & DRCOVER
Edited by Jackie Booe, MS Ed and D'Ivoire Johnson

This title is also available as an eBook on ebookministry.com
and at a discount for 501C3 and Ministry purchase.

Over 75 Scriptures in this book are identified in the Scripture
Reference Section, and are a part of many noted translations.

FOR MORE INFORMATION ABOUT
*DID GOD MAKE YOU HIS NEXT
CONSTRUCTION SITE?*

www.ebookministry.com

Dedicated to my
Supportive Husband and Children,
Mother, Father, Siblings, Aunts, Uncles, Cousins, Friends,
Business Associates, and divine encounters of Angels and
Prayer Warriors for supporting me, scolding and molding me
and Loving me most of all along this journey.

And a special Thank You to all of Gods specially
appointed to pour into my life over the years....
Apostle Savannah, Pastor Jones, Monsignor Ray East,
Bishop Bronner, Pastor Johnson, Pastor Clint Brown and
most of all My Mother, Apostle Veronica F. Best and Father,
Elder Mayo A Best Jr.

Table of Contents

The Master Builder Has A Plan

God is the *Master Builder* and *the Owner* of all sites. It is He who brings in the developer, *The Holy Spirit*, to reside and assist you in the preparation of the infrastructure of your site. When we first think about ourselves as a construction site, we need to think about the fact that the Lord has to choose a site to build on. We are just like a blank canvas ready for the creation of a masterpiece of fine architecture which will house God's spirit, His purpose and His power – A church if you will. All of this potential is within each and every one of us, just waiting to be discovered by us and refined by Him. Yet, just like any other structure, before we can build, we must first conduct a feasibility study. That means we have to understand Gods best and most useful purpose for ourselves. The first thing we need to do is assess a site for cost and figure out if the site is worth God choosing as a place to build. Much like raw land must be properly graded prior to the building of any structure, this inevitably will come with a cost. In the development of our purpose this cost would be considered sacrifice. So, then, the first thing we need to do, in our pursuit of purpose, is assess our site for cost. – What are we willing to sacrifice, to give up and to change, in order to become God's architectural masterpiece? This question is often most difficult to answer because we have drifted so far away from God's original purpose for our lives, such that to consider being transformed by faith often renders us fearful and seemingly immovable. Some of us have gotten so comfortable in the general flow of things that we are hesitant to sacrifice this perceived comfort without knowing and understanding that Gods blueprint for our lives is far better than any comforts we could ever obtain for ourselves.

We should consider all the cost that would be involved, and the fact that with God, we have a site that was paid for in advance. FEAR is the essential obstacle that must be removed from our lives if we are to become God's architectural masterpiece and construction site. Faith and fear cannot coexist within the same place. You must tackle fear and ultimately remove your doubts prior to breaking ground. The good news is that fear can be defeated by gaining a defined understanding of God's purpose for you. Once you understand your purpose, and establish your commitment and sacrifice necessary, productivity and prosperity are not far behind. The bible says that the Kingdom of God is within you. Do you know your worth to God? Is there a mansion inside of you?

Our complete plans were Paid-In-Full, just as if we are the Prime Real Estate belonging to God with the blood of Jesus Christ. The Bible tells us that God knew you before He formed you in your mothers' womb. This should be encouragement that the same God who allowed his son to make the ultimate sacrifice with his blood and life has chosen to value you as Prime Real Estate. Your personal sacrifice and commitment that you will make is rewarded by Custom plans that allow you to gain access to pick only the best, top of the line wood, framing, drywall, windows, foundation, and all that you would ever need to put into what you want to build? Jesus paid the price with His blood; to give you nothing but the best before you even thought yourself worthy; as proof of his unfailing love for all whom accept his salvation.

When I was coming up as a child, I did not have a lot of self-confidence in myself. I did not believe I was pretty nor had any value to anyone outside of my immediate family. I was always concerned about what others thought of me and I had low self-esteem. There was one thing that I never had to do without and that was love. I was always shown love from all the members of my family, and I realize now that it was all the love and support that was being poured into me that shaped my love and caring attitude toward others. In my earlier years I did not value the site God had given me, nor did I understand HIS love or sacrifice at that time. I was being used and abused by so many others that I felt like I was never going to be accepted by some and that I would always be left trying to please others. When I started going to church on my own and wanted my life to change, I began to notice that there was something special about me. I began to believe the "special" that I had to offer and that I was somebody. All I had to do was believe in his power to create in me whatever I wanted. I began to believe that ALL of my desires could and would be met if I gained a closer relationship with the Giver and not just the Gifts. I began to see myself as Prime Real Estate that would be built into something beautiful over time. I knew what some of my weaknesses were and believed it did not matter anymore. I began to believe that I could be that business woman that could run my own business and help a lot of people, and that was what I set out to do. All I did was make a decision and give my life to God as my commitment with obedience to him, not truly having the full understanding, but trusting in the love that I was told He had for me.

Can you trust Him? **Proverbs 3:5, 6** tells us to "Trust in the Lord with all your heart and lean not to your own understanding; acknowledge Him, and He will make all your paths straight."

We have to assess the quality of our site and the structure of how we are built. **Luke 6:48,** "He is like a man building a house, which is dug down deep and laid the foundation on rock. When a flood came, the torrent struck that house, but could not shake it because it was well built." God chooses you and all you have to do is understand that *He is the Master Builder*. When God chooses you as His next construction site, you have to know that we were already pre-platted and pre-planned for God's Glory and pleasure.

The next thing we think about is the location. We are told by real-estate experts that your location is significant to your success. God may consider your site Prime Real Estate for him. God may consider your site one of the best construction sites for His purpose to be fulfilled. He looks at the very state of our current site and our surroundings. Living in a place or working in a place that has someone or people that may, as we say, "need a little more Jesus in their life," is when you become Prime Real Estate, because that is where He can use YOU best.

There are times when I was in a place that I did not understand at the time, was exactly where God could use me the most. I did hair as a child and young adult and realize now that the very work that I did was bringing smiles to faces and allowing me to pour into them words of encouragement day after day. There were many women who told me after their hair treatment that they felt like they had just had a therapy session. My ministry was to listen and promote positive and sometimes chastising words that would always be from my heart and the Holy Spirit. I really did not understand my ministry of Hair until later. I have uplifted those with broken hearts, helped grieving mothers and siblings, inspired women to start their own businesses, spoke life into a depressed situation, and helped to give constructive criticism that has changed lives. I am still reminded by some people; words that I may have forgotten that have had an impact on their life years ago. There is one woman that told me later that she was right in the middle of a temptation to commit suicide and I called and she said that I spoke life back into her; not knowing at the time what God had just done. This was the platform that he chose to use for me to reach children and women of all ages from the time I was 12 years old until I was about 28. You begin to realize that God can and will use you in whatever place you are in. Right here is where you can become the catalyst to bring HIM Glory. In **Isaiah 61:1** the word says, "The spirit of the Lord is on me, because the Lord has appointed me to preach good news to the poor. He has sent me to bind up the brokenhearted, to proclaim freedom for the captives and release from darkness for the prisoners."

We have to understand that when God makes a selection and chooses you, we must accept it as an awesome opportunity and feel privileged to honor the sacrifice of Jesus and the price He paid for us. In **Revelations 4:11** the word says, "You created everything, and it is for your pleasure that they exist and were created." From the beginning of the word, God created us in His image and for His Glory. From the first book of the Bible to the last book of the Bible, He has called it good that He created us. **Psalm 149:4,** "The Lord takes pleasure in His people." God did not need to make you and me; He chose to make you.

So let's take a minute to understand what we have! We don't just have a builder; we have God as the Master Builder. The word *Architekton* was used in Ancient Greece and derived from the Greek word for Master Builder. In ancient times, the Master Builder is trained in all phases of design and construction. In Greece, the builders said it was the art of building according to principles which are determined, not merely by the ends the edifice is intended to serve, but by the consideration of beauty and harmony. He is the overseer of the entire project, from concept and design through construction. The high standards and responsibilities of a Master Builder are unique. He has extreme passion and dedication. He is committed to excellence. Our Master Builder can make design changes in the middle of a project, still understanding all the dynamics and conditions that exist. He is able to make adjustments to navigate the plans, while accommodating the end result of His plan. "For I know the plans I have for you," declares the Lord in **Jeremiah 29:11**, "plans to prosper you and not to harm you, plans to give you hope and a future." Isn't it wonderful that we have someone that understands the very make up of each and every one of us? God operates all of our development to bring us into a prosperous future.

When you accept that you are His construction site, He will begin to collaborate with contractors and tradesman to fix all of the problems. Whether you are in need of a roofer to guard and repair your shelter from outside or harsh elements; a plumber to decide the water and life you pour into your home and the excrement that is allowed to flow from it; or an electrician that is needed to help you decide where there is a lack of energy being distributed at the appropriate level of current to operate your appliances in the best and efficient light possible. He has the respect of all who are appointed by Him to produce His end result of your masterpiece. He has the ability to deliberately alter a situation in your life that is targeted to give resolution to any of the deficiencies that may

be apparent at that time.

Your On-Site Counselor/Supervisor

He provides you with an on-site Supervisor and Counselor, One who knows how to communicate beyond your understanding. This is the Holy Spirit, and God gives us the Holy Spirit in whom we can have rest. **John 4:16-17,** "And I will ask the Father and He will give you another Counselor to be with you forever – the Spirit of truth. The world cannot accept him nor knows him. But you know him, for He lives with you and will be in you." The Holy Spirit is here to convict us when we have a need that needs to be addressed. The Holy Spirit transforms us by providing us with the gifts of the spirit. **Galatians 5:22-23** "But the evidence of the Spirit is love, joy, peace, longsuffering, kindness, goodness, faithfulness, gentleness and self-control." Imagine being loved in spite of your short-comings to the extent that the very act of your overcoming them gives glory to God. The Holy Spirit is there as a seal that guarantees us eternal life with God and as an edification of us to our peers that supports the power

that has been given to us. It empowers us to be a witness and

speak boldly for the Lord through the conquered trials that are

achieved through unexplainable terms that are only

demonstrated with the help of the Holy Spirit.

Everything you need to be perfected and all that you desire

has already been Paid-In-Full and you have a counselor who is

there to guide you 24 hours each day, 7 days a week, always

on call for you to speak to the Master Builder in a language

that He understands. The Counselor will go to Him on your

behalf when an alteration is needed or whenever you need

help to complete His work. 1 **Corinthians 2:12,** "For we have

not received the Spirit of the World but the Spirit who is from

God, that we may understand what God has freely given us."

God gives you the Holy Spirit so that you can understand that

which is too difficult for human ability to understand. He

gives us supernatural understanding to overcome all situations and adversaries that may come to destroy our efforts.

I have been in situations that were certain to cause me harm or stress and out of nowhere, I had spoken a word or words that were stated from my lips without effort or concentration that only could have come from the Holy Spirit. I did not have the complete understanding or the technical training to be able to figure out the reasoning behind my comments, but they were spoken at the right time, with the right amount of confidence and posture that would allow me to be delivered from situations that were inevitable according to man's eyes. There have been many situations where I did not want to face some of the major or even minor problems that I had going on in my life. I would pick a day and decide that I would deal with all of the problems that I was dealing with and all of the people that I was enduring. Several times after committing to deal with whatever they were going to bring to me in the form of arguments, chastisements or even venting; I did not so much as get a whimper or hint of aggression or chastising tone. I believe that sometimes, God wants us to trust him and he will show up when you least expect him to. All of my preparation was never needed. I put myself through more in my mind than the actual individuals I had to deal with. There is a joke that goes "If you want to tell God a joke, tell him your plans".

Another experience I had with the supernatural power of God was when I was driving along a winding road on a one lane road. I could barely see the road because of the pouring rain and as I was driving, I tried to make a turn to the right and the car started to drift left as I seemed to lose control of the car. I felt helpless and could see the light pole and other cars that were coming closer as I slid sideways toward them. All I could think of was that I needed help and fast. I screamed out "Jesus!" From the depth of my very soul I needed him to help me as I felt like I could have been seriously injured or even

killed by the impact that was about to occur. Suddenly, the

car jerked, straightened out and came to a slow and peaceful

stop. In the middle of that earthly storm, my heart cried out

and I believe Jesus himself heard my cry and moved

supernaturally to my aid. If not Jesus, the very power of His

name demanded the protection and his angels to protect me. It

was just like I would do for my son when he was riding his

bike losing control and was about to crash; I would position

his bike upward and steady for him to continue on with

confidence that I was there to protect him from failing. This is

the feeling I have about Gods provisions that He has put in

place for us. There is a song that was released called "Jesus

take the wheel". It brought me to tears thanking of his

goodness over twenty years later.

Psalm 127:1, "Unless the Lord builds the house, its

builder's labor in vain. Unless the Lord watches over the city, the watchmen stand guard in vain." When you trust God to handle the details, and you trust the Spirit that He has provided you with, you have the upper hand in all your efforts. Giving God full control over your development builds the confidence that is necessary to push through your obstacles and work hard, knowing your efforts are not in vain. We need God to use us for His Glory and while you are in the process, the enemy will try to trick you into thinking that you are not worthy: You are chosen as His personal construction site! You are bought and paid for with the Blood of Jesus! Fight against the temptation to accept the world's labels of your worth and be determined to receive your complete and perfect build! Accept what God wants to do with you and stop fighting it! Make sure you completely embrace the unique design He gave you. In all your flaws, imperfections and in-abilities, God can and will perfect that which pleases Him.

Isaiah 43:1, "Fear Not, for I have redeemed you; I have summoned you by name; you are mine!"

To state clearly, **1Peter 2:9** exclaims "But you are a chosen people, a royal priesthood, a Holy nation, a people belonging to God, that you may declare the praises of him who called you out of darkness into His wonderful light!" It is in some of the darkest places that Light shines the brightest. It is in the darkest soil that some of the reddest roses are produced. Your light will shine so bright inside and out that others will see the Glory of God in your construction site that will illuminate Gods love for you because of your current presence and what you have been through.

When I was younger I was challenged by a lot of people whom I trusted that took advantage of my naive nature and kindness; leaving me confused and left feeling depressed and broken hearted. However, when God builds or rebuilds, He takes you on as His next construction site and that is when He gets the glory. When He is done, it will be revealed what God has built for His Glory. I am a living; walking and enthusiastic person who's testimony can help those that are going through the same storms that I have overcome. I give a testimony of how I got over and got through all of the trials I endured and came through with a passion to pull others out of that state faster and stronger than they were because of it.

When God's Glory comes, you never have to wonder if this is the work of God or if this is the Work of Man! You are no longer man made but refined as a Gift by God himself! He wants to see His Glory in all the earth! He is looking for us to ask Him and to call on Him to be our Master Builder. After you submit to Him, you must welcome the Holy Spirit right now and begin or continue to allow Him to work in you and through you for yourself, and for God's Glory.

Sometimes God Picks A Restoration Project For His Next Construction Site

Sometimes God wants to use a site that is already built. It might have broken out windows and the shell might look a little rough with dents and dings, but it is still holding on. It may have many imperfections inside of it from all of the wear and tear of people coming into and out of it. This is the wear that comes from misuse of what God intended for you. The carpet may be torn and worn and people may have written and inscribed a few nasty or distasteful things on your walls. People may have left their baggage in your heart. It might have clutter on the inside and have mix-match and mixed up used furniture on the inside from all of the conflict and unfinished ideas left uncompleted or undone. Don't you know that no matter what people have deposited on the inside of you, no matter what you look like on the inside or outside, and no matter how bad the site is that God has to work with, He can fix it?

All a Master Builder needs is the foundation that He created in His image and He can and will restore you to even better than before. He can take a restoration project to better than you ever dreamed possible. He works beyond the very realm of our understanding, because His thoughts are not our thoughts.

Just as man did not understand why God would allow one of the most notable men in the Bible (Job) to be tested by the Devil with permission to cause Job to go through so much pain and heartache; endure physical hardships to his health and appearance, lose family members and all of his assets; only to bless him mightily one hundred fold what he had lost and endured in his latter days. It is in this magnificent story that I was led to read without interruption of phones or daily family issues, while sitting on a quiet outside pool deck that I came to the understanding that there is truly a purpose in your pain. Job has a testimony that will cause you to understand that centuries later God could use Job's tests as fuel that many

people need today to carry on through trials knowing that

sometimes it is not all coming from evil; God could be trying

to teach you and others through the pain. I developed a saying

that goes, *"Sometimes God orchestrates chaos in a strategic*

manner to achieve His end result!"

Just listen to **Psalm 147:5**, which says, "How great is our

Lord! His power is absolute! His understanding is beyond

comprehension." Don't allow whoever you call the

adversaries in your life ("the Devil, Satan, diabolical or evil

spirits or spiteful people) make you feel that just because you

have lost things or been used, abused, and or battered through

life's circumstances that God can't build a mansion inside of

you right where you stand! As the Master Builder, He alone

has the power to create a priceless gem in you, which allows

him to build you up on the very same foundation that He has

already put in place.

He will replace your old windows with new ones that only allow things on the inside to be seen by others when you want them to. He protects your soul with a special brand of UV protection that allows you to see clearly through them from the inside out, yet it will not allow harmful things to penetrate through from the outside. He can replace the front door to your home with a solid wood door and dead bolt guarded by the Holy Spirit and protected by His Angels; they will guard your home site from those people that you once allowed to come in and out at will, bringing only destructive thoughts and actions to you. He will clean out the inside and remove all the clutter and debris that has been deposited in you by others and even by you. He will replace the ordinary drywall with reinforced materials that can withstand more pressure than ever before. He will give you new floors and carpet that will withstand the footprints that you allow to enter without leaving any blemishes, marks, or residue on the inside. He will give you a brand new paint job and a brand new look. He will build everything up in you with the Power of God left inside!

Trust God and you will no longer need to trust in human wisdom to decorate and bring beauty to your home. He may send you counsel and you will find refuge from His direction. You must only trust in God's wisdom to orchestrate the design of every aspect of you. When you allow God to use you as His vessel and for His joy, no mistakes are made, only powerful lessons learned that allow you to embrace the beauty in being adorned with the perfection of the Holy Spirit to guide you. When you decide to allow God to use you, then you begin to operate in a spirit of understanding and belief that God IS changing you and your life. You start to understand that He is guiding your thoughts and moving your mindset from having uncertainty about most things you have done on the inside, to having a clarity and confidence about the decisions you make with God's vision for you and your home.

He will redecorate the inside of you first and restore your body

from the inside out. He will also give you a bold spirit to

declare *that's enough* and set you free from having and

allowing others to bring all of their junk, debris, and clutter

into your life. **2 Corinthians 12:9**, "But He said to me, my

grace is sufficient for you, for my power is made perfect in

weakness. Therefore I will boast all the more gladly about my

weaknesses, so that Christ's power may rest on me." All you

have to do is ask for His help, and He will empower you to

stop letting others wear you down and wear you out. **1**

Corinthians 16:13, "Be on your guard; stand firm in the faith,

be men of courage; be strong." God's provisions and the Holy

Spirit will help you to stop letting others inscribe their nasty

labels of you, or other hurtful things, in to your heart and your

soul. Once you completely receive that God has chosen you

to be restored to even better than you ever were before, the enemy will come. Haters, people that are jealous of you, those that covet the things you have will be at your door as soon as God starts your repair and restoration process. So get ready and stay ready with His word and the promises made over your life. For Joshua said unto them in **Joshua 10:25,** "Fear not, nor be dismayed, be strong and of good courage: for thus shall the Lord do to all your enemies against whom you fight."

I want to share a little something with you. I want to share some of the things that have come against me, things that have been done to me, what people have talked about me, and how they've betrayed me and let me down. I have been brought to some of the lowest points in my life trying to help others and putting my trust in mankind. God has used some of my biggest, worldly losses to be a part of His plan to bring restoration not only to myself, but to others. A lot of people seem to believe that I don't have and have never had to go through anything in my life. I have been used by both man and woman. I've been lied to and talked about. I have had those that I truly trusted and loved steal from me. I have made investments for people and made them a lot of money, but none for myself. Some talked about me while others encouraged me to go forward. I lost a home of eight years, had repossessed cars, and lost many of life's little conveniences and a lot of things that I took for granted. Some of the same people that used to cherish everything I did for them in their life as one of their only positive impressions they had experienced in a long time began to admonish me. They acted as if I was a different person because of the circumstances. Some people expressed doubt in the truthfulness of my statements. Most of all, I never thought my integrity would ever be questioned, much less that I would have to justify every dollar. **1 Peter 4:12** "Therefore let those who suffer according to God's will entrust their souls to a faithful Creator while doing good." We are going to suffer at times, but don't let your persecution stop you from praising

God. Sufferings are not just for the evil, bad or sinful people.

You will learn through your sufferings and persecution.

There are times when you will feel like you are under so

much pressure and under attack from the enemy. You are

going to have to give praises to God before you come into

your problems. He has to bring problems that help build a

stronger prayer life and relationship with God. There is power

in your praise that guards off the enemy and brings action

from his angels to your aid in times of distress. My husband

always says "Don't get ready, stay ready." He is speaking

about life and ultimately this applies to us in the Spirit realm

of being ready and girded with Gods armor through prayer and

praises from the inside of ourselves. Praise him and stay in his

presence.

In submission to Him, "Lord Help," I cried out! But the

storms still came. You see sometimes God picks a restoration project for His next construction site! Sometimes He needs a site that is worn, torn, battered, or even in the middle of a hurricane. When I lost my house, I was strengthened because I knew He had chosen me as His next construction site. I was being refined through all of the pressures and fires leading up to the point of sale. It became a mission for me and a constant and consistent fuel for me to help many others going through the same battles. Not only did I lose my own home, but I lost my parents' home of over twenty years in the middle of the real- estate crisis. I also lost the home of one of my most cherished family members who had 40 years of memories tied to it.

You have to know that I have had some very long and weary nights of pain and feeling downtrodden and in despair, feeling that I had unintentionally betrayed the trust of some of the people that were closest to my heart. There were family members, friends, and even private investors that trusted me to give increase to their lives and not alter the very lifeline that most families find shelter and comfort in. "BUT GOD!"

Jeremiah 30:17 it says, "But I will restore you to health and heal your wounds, declares the Lord, because you are called an outcast, Zion for whom no one cares."

I felt like I was the one that had been providing them with most of the answers to all of their questions pertaining to real estate and now I was being cast out as a person without good intentions. I was told that I should have known what was going to happen and I should have seen the signs. It happened so fast and I could not recover from the market crash in the housing market no matter what I tried to do to make a deal happen, I was never able to close another transaction. All of the false concern for my family and for my personal well-being had all but disappeared from any of my conversations with these individuals. I felt bad and did not like all the things that were being said about me by some.

How many of you reading this right now recognize that this wasn't a pleasant experience to have others ridicule and question my very integrity? I felt like an outcast, even in my own home. I had been a contributor in my own home for so long and always had been able to help my family and my husband by contributing financially and mentally.

My home and all the things I wanted for my children and my husband were taken away. My husband and children trusted the decisions I made to help us live a comfortable life that was no longer very comfortable or convenient. We went without power and my husband gave up a good business trusting in me at that time. I often asked myself how many people could I let down?

And then a prayer and a promise from God began to change everything. I remember sitting alone on the side of my bed and asking God to speak to me.   During all the trials that I had been through, I was dealing with a specific home and continually asking God to help me, I began to pray for God to

help those that were affected by my actions receive comfort

from Him and know that no matter what the outcome was, that

they would be able to see God in the middle of their situation

and see the God that still resided in me. I asked him to let

them see that I was the same and that my integrity was still

intact. I prayed that their hardships would be over and that

any hardship that I had caused would be taken away and that

He would get the glory. I asked him to let me find a way to

repay everyone and make everything right. I remember Him

saying as plain as someone that was sitting right next to me, in

a loud and clear voice from within, " I have a purpose for the

pain that you feel you are causing, it is my will not yours and I

am that I am and always will be. I am proud of you and you

are my child. You will go through much more, but in the end,

I will bless you and you will be a blessing to many." I began

to understand through his expressions of thought that

continued to linger in my mind that there was more to what was going on than I could see with my own carnal vision.

It was during my greatest afflictions that I developed my deepest relationship with God. I understood more and more the decrees that he has set aside for me. David said in **Psalm 119:71** "It was good for me to be afflicted, that I might learn thy decrees." The biggest battle that most of us face is in our own minds. Our mind is the biggest battlefield on Earth. There are a lot of situations that we allow ourselves to be defeated in because of our lack of self-control or self-discipline. When you go into a situation with a feeling of fear or doubt, you allow the adversary to gain the upper hand and position themselves over you with confidence based on your posture and fear evidenced in your speech, body language and inconsistent ability to exude confidence. In some instances we create situations and doubt of others; we assess situations in a negative light and always view life from a negative perspective no matter how things really are. This type of

person always views the glass as half empty instead of half

full. They conquer themselves before anyone ever comes

against them; they stay in a place that is against themselves.

The more I began to understand that I have the Master Builder

to lean on began to empower me and my way of thinking.

Let's get this straight. When I have the confidence and the

excitement in what I am doing and what it is that I am working

on, the more positive things start to happen with a lot less

effort. We have a Master Builder with all the plans, where

everything must work together for the good of those that love

the Lord. I was reminded that He is a God who can help

restore me and build upon all the brokenness and failed

dreams I had. **Psalm 54:4,** "Surely God is my help; the Lord

is the one who sustains me!" We have each been appointed

through our struggles, to pull strength from His word, because

we trust in His unfailing love and power. We should ask him

to "restore to me the joy of your salvation and grant me a willing spirit, to sustain me." **Psalm 51:12;** If you claim to believe in the Word of God, then you have the Power to be sustained through any trial. If you are not sure about your relationship with God, or even who God is or represents in your life. Be on notice that you are also given a promise and the tools to find out the truth for yourself. In **Jeremiah 29:13** he says, "You will seek me and find me when you seek me with all your heart."

God says in 2 **Corinthians 1:8** says, "We do not want you to be uninformed, brothers, about the hardships we suffered in the province of Asia. We were under great pressure for beyond our ability to endure, so that we despaired even of life!" This just confirmed the saying that there is nothing new under the sun. Centuries ago man had the same feelings as I did. I began to default on agreements and lose more and more property. I tried to hold on and lost all of our savings trying to get back on top. People began to treat me as if I made the market crash and it was my entire fault! I felt like I didn't even want to go on or be here anymore at times. Nevertheless it says in **Psalm 73:26,** <u>"My flesh and my heart may fail, but God is the strength of my heart and my portion forever!"</u> They were treating me like I wasn't the same person that had been blessing them for years, month after month. Wisdom has shown me the true character and faith of a person is not shown until something happens to make it reveal itself. **Psalm 69:4,** <u>"Those who hate me without reason, outnumber the hairs on my head; many are my enemies without cause; those who seek to destroy me. I am forced to restore what I did not steal."</u> This spoke to me so loudly. And I began to think about all of the power I felt I had lost and gave too much power to those thoughts. Then, the literal power went off, my swimming pool broke, I lost a vehicle, and the AC went out in the house in the middle of the summer! This was really symbolic of the fact that everything that I was worried about was becoming more of my problem and I was becoming a bigger restoration project day by day. Thank God I had a supportive husband and family, a praying Mother and Father, friends, aunts, uncles and many other prayer warriors that had even a glimpse of some of the things that I was going through.

We serve a God that likes to work the impossibilities. I had a family member to tell me that I was always selling pipe dreams to people! "No!" I said emphatically, "I still believe in the Power of a God that works beyond my understanding. I still believe in the God that can do all things and gets the Glory just for being the orchestrator of things that seem impossible for us to accomplish." In order for you to receive the blessings that God has set aside for you, you must have the faith that he can do the impossible. You have to declare those things that aren't as though they are already achieved. This principle is being taught in many different faiths and under disguised principals of the basic laws of the Universe. When

you believe something to be able to be done that ultimately is

not a normal capable action, you activate the God given ability

that each one of us has been given to reign with dominion over

all the earth with the ability to achieve greater works than that

of Jesus himself. In **John 4:4** Jesus assures us "Verily, verily,

I say unto you, He that believeth on me, the works that I do

shall he do also; and greater works than these shall he do;

because I go unto my Father."

The more things that began to happen, the more I began to

be empowered that there was a lesson in the loss that

empowered me to stand!   God kept telling me to just "Stand

and know that I am God!" He started to fight the battles for

me and all I had to do was to be still and confident in His

abilities and the power of His word. He began to reveal more

and more to me in the middle of the storms that kept coming.

I could feel myself growing stronger and stronger. Things that used to bother me didn't faze me and the things that used to make me cringe didn't even move me to an emotion of anything other than a feeling of *been there and done that* or *already heard that before*.

He began to have me release all the things that I was holding on to one by one. We have to let hurt feelings go, past issues and anything that you are not proud of, and just hold on to God alone. We have to depend on the power He has placed inside of ourselves to fix those things, and mend hearts and minds that man can't change. You see, we have to look to God for the restoration of our spirit and of our hearts. Don't be angry with God, when you are having a hard time. You are not being abandoned by Him. **Hebrews 6:10** says "God is not unjust; he will not forget your work and the love you have shown him as you have helped his people and continue to help them." Our job is just to believe that what Jesus did when He died for me and for us was enough. We just need to believe with complete certainty that we are everything that we want to be and allow the restoration through the love of God to occur.

And then He began to restore me through obedience and allowed the restoration process to occur through the very people that were part of the pain. I began to believe there was a purpose in the pain. You see the redemption is already done. God will give you the Spirit of Understanding.

He will show you how your understanding of situations is so far off the mark of His plan by some of the blessings He allows you to see, as a result of things you thought were meant for evil that were in fact used as a tool to set the stage for something great. An assumed loss of a home to someone that I truly love and care about became one of the biggest blessings and testimonies that one of my family members has shared with so many people. God uses you in some instances through chaos that is not always about you. He will begin to teach you through your pain. As my saying goes, *"Sometimes God orchestrates chaos in a strategic manner to achieve His end result!"*

When God begins to grant you the wisdom to understand that it is not all about you, you can begin to be healed and restored to even better than before. When God began to show up for all of them, He began to show me that I needed to hang up the cape I had been holding on to. You can't be all things for everybody. Your job is to live YOUR best YOU. God himself is a jealous God. Make sure you are not playing God to someone and ultimately blocking a blessing that God is trying to provide. Sometimes God has chosen multiple restoration sites that He alone wants to get the glory for the restoration and replenishment of. In **John 14:2**, "in my Father's house are many mansions: if it were not so, I would have told you. I go to prepare a place for you." Don't keep trying to avoid the struggles, ask God for the wisdom and strength behind them.

We can get in the way of God's plan by always trying to assist those that are trying to overcome obstacles that He may want to get the Glory for. Make sure you pray about each and every situation before you act. Even if it is done with a good heart, just ask God for his directions. God says "I am that I am" and He does not need our help to restore or replenish someone. You are only to be used as a tool at His request. Remember that you are a vessel to be used at His discretion. He wants us to come to him at all times. Even when your heart tells you to do something, pray on it first. Give pause to quick and unwitty actions that have not been thought through or ordered. If you are the first person someone thinks about and calls on when they need help instead of God, even if they are your adult children or a closest friend, that's a problem. God wants us to be totally dependent on him first and not man, even if it is your mother, a spouse, friend, or anyone you count on before going to God. I not only had to hang up my cape, but I had to tell them all that I did it and not worry about their responses or feelings about it.

In **2 Chronicles 24:12,** it states "The King hired subcontractors like masons and carpenters to restore the Lord's temple that specialized in bronze and iron to repair the temple." Your body is a temple provided to you by God to be respected and taken care of with diligence and respect. You have been created in His image with abilities even greater than that of this world and His son. Sometimes you will be able to give life with the things you thought had no purpose. You are a marvel in the kingdom of God; every person you meet has a place in your life. There are NO chance encounters. You are not only a temple for and of God; you are a vessel to be used with all the power and might that your inheritance brings.

You have to respect the journey of restoration and trust Him to complete any work that He starts and that which He has begun. Most times it is the journey that is priceless not the destination! All of the people that come against you must know that you are trusting in God with all that you have. When you feel that you have no more to give or you find yourself weary, speak the prayer in **Psalm 119:116** where it says, "Lord, sustain me as you promised that I may live. Do not let my hope be crushed!" When you call on God and ask for His help, it is a demonstration of both faith and humility. You will begin to feel free when you walk in that awareness with courage and confidence in the Lord's ability to do just what He has said.

Bless the Lord at all times. **2 Samuel 22:33** "God is my strong refuge and has made my way blameless." He is your strength and your strong tower of where you can find rest and He does not hold you responsible for anything past your repentance. The same God that has supplied all of your needs will and can supply the needs of those that call on you. Are you representing this to those that call on you? Are you leading them into that place of rest and confidence in the same Father that we all have access to? You are commissioned to do this. **Psalm 31:3,** "Since you are my rock and my fortress, for the sake of your name, lead me and guide me."

We serve an awesome God! **Psalm 126:5 says,** "Those who sow in tears will reap with songs of joy." Don't worry about a few tears you shed over the site you currently are working with. You can have a joy that the world can't create or give you when God replaces your frown with a smile. And the best part of all is whatever joy God gives you can't be taken away by anyone in the world. I always say *"Don't let your current circumstances dictate your joy!"* *"Time and circumstance changes all things, even if it's only the perception of it."*

If God chooses you as His next Restoration Project, you should thank him right now! "you know someone that you feel has been chosen, please encourage him or her to trust God as you would. If He can do it for me, then He can do the same for anyone. There is no mountain high enough that God can't help you to get over. Start giving Him praise for what He is doing inside of you and in your life right now. Exalt Him in your actions and in your obedience to His Word. When you do this, you will walk with confidence, speak with courage and be infused with the wisdom at the time you have need, and even begin to walk in the true anointing and power that only God can provide. **Psalm 71:8,** "My mouth is filled with your praise, declaring your splendor all day long!" Trust Him all day and in everything that you do and say, singing praise to Him in all things. Give your past no attention and go forward with the understanding that it is in your forward praise and awareness that you can be restored to a new place and have a new life. Your site might be a restoration project, but when He gets your mindset in alignment with His, He does not care about your past. When you begin to operate under the true anointing that He intends for your life. He will refine your thoughts, your ways, your steps, your responses, and your current intentions. Just as gold in its earlier stages, is full of different alloys that need to be removed by refinement through applying intense heat or a strategic chemical processes in order for its complete and pure element to be revealed; you will be refined through the applied pressures that will remove elements of imperfections and unwanted substances from your site. When the process is complete, no one cares what was there in the beginning. After all has fallen off and the gold has been poured into its perfect mold, its brilliance shines and the result is magnificent and valued more than ever before to anyone who views it. Hold on to the thoughts of his design and purpose in all you do and go through. To Him your present has purpose and can be built to a finer glory and majesty than you have ever thought possible.

A Sub-Contractor Can Assess Your Soil

Once God has chosen your site to build, we have to assess our soil to make sure it is ready for God to start. When you are primed and ready in Gods eyes he will send you individuals that are purposed to bring His will for your life to fruition. At times we may have to call in a qualified subcontractor to determine if the soil we have is fortified with enough strength and minerals to hold the foundation. We have to assess the foundation and all of the things that we have put into it. We have to have an honest assessment of every aspect of ourselves. *You have to know what you are made of.* When the foundation is laid on top of good soil that is ready for the foundation to be built, it is then that the foundation will not crack or crumble, shift or even sink, be unwavering and stanch in its completion. Allow only those who are appointed by Him to encourage, uplift, or build you up in your past or those that you trust to give you an honest and worthy assessment of your soil. You have to have a qualified person to help you and hold you accountable for correction.   Is your soil fine and thin or thick and rich in what God has put in place to support all that goes into it? When you are determined to move according to Gods will for you, it is imperative that you get an honest assessment of what you may have to adjust from someone that you hold in high regard that exemplifies God, and has a relationship with him. Speak to others that seem to be connected and always take their information back to God first before making any adjustments. It is your soil that determines what type of structure God can build on it in the first place.

Do you have someone in your life that can be totally honest with you? Make sure you have someone in your life that is willing to tell you that your soil may have an impurity, even when you think it is fine. Will you listen to them? Are you allowing yourself to be approachable? You need to have someone who will hold you to a higher standard and push you to fertilize and take out even the small impurities. Someone who is willing to help you, even aggravate you and refine you with gentle and yet steady pressure when necessary that can lead you out of a dark place into your best light. With a little effort, you can remove anything from your soil that displeases God and even yourself. Allow the intent of your heart and your soul to have a distinct purpose in life which becomes intent on pleasing God and the Holy Spirit. When you accept a sub-contractor and allow God to bring in subcontractors, He can allow them to pour in to your soil the humic substances of life allowing your soil to bear miraculous fruit and causing a harvest of everlasting life! You will rest in the evidence that Jesus died so that you can have life and have it more abundantly. He wants to cause our soil to be an example of His love in the excellence that He can create. We are washed in the blood and sealed with His Spirit. We have to allow God to till our soil.

He warns us about what we put into the soil of our lives. **Hosea 10:13**, "But you have planted wickedness, you have reaped evil, you have eaten the fruit of deception. Because you have depended on your own strength and on your many warriors,--" we have a choice in what we choose to infuse our soil with. In essence, we can reap destruction, trouble, and wickedness. Or we can allow the Holy Spirit that resides in us to guide us to the very fertilizer and necessary substances that will sow peace into our lives and the lives of others that will rise up a harvest of righteousness.

We have to make sure that we pack our soil with the steady content that will endure whatever weight is put on top of it. If it is not compact with reinforcements and supporting material, the foundation won't be properly constructed. God requires us to be diligent when we are in preparation of what God is going to do for us. You must learn to take refuge in the counsel of others which are God's sub-contractors with special expertise in areas where you lack wisdom or understanding. God wants you to allow yourself to be fortified with His love and study to show yourself approved. God brings those who will teach you, lead you, or guide you. Your efforts to cultivate the soil you have will be blessed with the Holy Spirit and approved with a stamp of God's anointing. Do not be ashamed of any of your short comings at the beginning of your development. Let go of your entire preset and pre-determined understanding of your vision and let God measure the vision He has planned for you..

Once you have truly done your due diligence by prayer and studying for your own personal understanding and God's vision has been made plain according to the interpretation He has placed in your heart, start out with the willingness to accept what He brings to you, and be willing to let go of what He takes from you, leaving you fortified by His grace and mercy. Start right where you stand and work toward the vision He has shown you without reservation or hesitation.

When you have allowed God to till your soil and you have begun to harvest your works for him, you will start to enjoy the new soil that has been cultivated for your new life to begin.

What Type Of Blueprint Plan Is Needed
For Your Site?

Now, you have accepted and understand the benefit of
allowing God to choose you as His next construction site, and
you have figured out what type of soil you must have to
complete a solid foundation. And you have chosen your team.
You have God as your Master Builder, the Holy Spirit as your
24/7 Developer Consultant, and Jesus, the architect who paid
for everything in full.

I believe you don't have to have a stock built home. You
are entitled to a custom built plan. When choosing a plan that
fits the characteristics of your site, it is better to make the
house fit the site, than the site fit the house. What types of
characteristics do you have? Are you talkative or the silent
type? Do you like being around people? What do you enjoy
doing? What are you good at doing? What do you enjoy
doing so much that is a service to someone that you would do
it for free? Are you bold or meek? Do you like bright colors

or neutral? God can incorporate your innermost desires and natural abilities into His plan for you! Don't limit the plan that God has for you. Don't underestimate His power to fulfill all of your dreams! If it is too small and you don't need help to achieve it or accomplish it, then it is not inspired by God. God wants us to reach for the stars and we are bound to land on the moon. When we are inspired with something that seems impossible to reach, it is then that you have to trust Him with all your heart. Most of us have fallen short of this very simple task. **Ephesians 3:20**, "Now unto Him that is able to do exceeding abundantly above all that we ask or think, according to the power that works within us."

This says a lot about the God we serve, yet we still question the abilities of God beyond what we feel we can obtain within our own efforts or knowledge of resources we have access to.

A few years ago; before Redbox as we know it to be, this is a movie box that dispenses movies with the use of a credit card that has since inception grown to a multi-million dollar business. I was in Miami Beach and had to drive 86 blocks from our hotel to find a Blockbuster store to rent a movie that we wanted to watch for the evening. I had an idea that I would create a machine that would dispense movies and place them in all the hotels and any place that would have access to people that would want to rent movies with an ease of access. I was stumped from moving forward because of the perceived impossible feat of creating the machine, needing engineers, needing a movie distribution network, software programmers and the list went on and on. I began to defeat my own vision by getting discouraged by my lack of resources to handle all the areas necessary to complete my vision. I was limiting Gods ability and the belief that everything under the sun belongs to him. I did not have the confidence that God was bigger than any needs I had.

I know now, after receiving my third gifted vision from God, that man's view of what I need and how much is needed to accomplish something is only man's view and in no way measures up to all of the ways that God has to solve each and every obstacle we come across or even small detail that needs to be met. I have lost ideas to my own fears and lack of trust in God. My father always says "God always has a ram in the bush" if we will just trust him to bring it. Now, I have aligned myself with the will that God has for me and will not allow any obstacle to move me from my goals. I can and will trust that God will provide every distinct detail, better than I could plan for. He has begun to put resources that are from the top of the market and blessed me with the contacts that have been willing to help me and share all of their resources that I have needed to achieve His vision for the ideas he has given me.

Everything that I thought I wanted is being expanded and has grown so far beyond my initial vision that the Magnitude of the vision has to be accomplished by Gods resources, which ultimately lends a testimony for His Glory alone. There is no one that could get any type of credit for what has already been accomplished. Every detail that has been afforded to me has come through channels I never dreamed of or had any knowledge of prior to the need. Most importantly, the people that I feel have been assigned to help me are unusually interested in my success, even to their own stated lack of understanding as to why they are even so compelled to help me. This happens when you obtain favor from God. **Psalm 40:4** says, "Blessed is the man who makes the Lord his trust." He will have someone call you with just what you are looking for and you may not know who to call. He will guide you to a website or company that may have a need to promote your product or purchase something you need to sell. When you begin to walk in Gods favor, everything you have a need for that aligns with his purpose for you will show up. If you have a product that you need to sell, there is always someone who needs that item. There is nothing that you need on earth that you are more than four people away from.

We have to begin to align our thoughts and our actions with the desires of our heart as if we know with all certainty that we are capable of achieving whatever we ask or want. Whatever plans you have, if they glorify God and His commands, you will succeed. He also says in **1 Kings 3:13**, "Moreover, I will give you what you have not asked for—both riches and honor –so that in your lifetime you will have no equal among Kings." Our God's plans for us are to give us not only what we want, but our innermost desires. Things you don't even have to speak out loud. When He builds you up, over time your own plans will evolve and change. You will mature into the place where you will learn to embrace the challenges that allow you to expose your hidden potential and treasures that you find can only be revealed through pressures of life. **Colossians 4:12,** "He is always wrestling in prayer for you, that you may stand firm in the Will of God, mature and fully assured." As you mature in your acceptance of the Will of God, you will begin to grow in areas you never knew possible. Find refuge in the plans God has for you and He will strengthen you when you are weak and carry you when you can't go any further. I have a little saying that goes, *when you can't go any farther, just take one more step; if you feel you can't do anymore, just pray and do some more.* The only excuses we have come from our own lack of faith. How many times have you heard stories of someone conquering something that was thought to be impossible with just one more try or one *last ditch effort?*

There is power in your push. Better stated is, *when you have done all you can do, you can decide to let God do the rest through you.* There is a story about a woman who had a terrible accident and was on life support and in a coma for three months with no response to anyone. The family was called in to make a decision about her direction and her life. They reluctantly chose to take her off life support and let her go because they were told she would never wake up. When the doctors removed the tube and shut off the life support, the woman woke up from what she felt had just been a deep sleep! Her eyes began to flutter and her speech immediately returned. God delivered her from the decision they had made. God showed them that He was her life support and her breathing tube, and that with God and Him alone, all things are possible. She has been giving testimony to this event in every place she can find a listening ear. Her testimony is that His goodness was sufficient even in her weakness. She is a living testimony for those that need a word against the will of negative or pessimistic people in their life. **Romans 15:32** "Then, by the will of God, I will be able to come to you with a joyful heart,

and we will be an encouragement to each other." He will take

the characteristics that make you unique and enhance them to

make His Glory shine through you. His blueprint for your life

is custom-made with perfection and the omniscient

perspective of each aspect of your life. So let His plans

manifest with excellence out of the pure Agape Love that He

wants to impart to you. Let them grow into a model showing

His fortitude and strength, "for when your endurance is fully

developed, you will be perfect and complete lacking in

nothing." **James 1:4**

Remember when God is designing your site and building

your house, the exterior is easy to change. Get interested with

how your inside is constructed. When your front door is open,

how does it look on the inside? Do you have anger residing in

your heart? Does envy set within your closets? Is

unforgiveness lingering within your thoughts creating

unhealthy patterns on your walls that leave them exposed for others to blatantly see? It is the interior that needs to be built with sterner stuff and most likely needs to be organized.

Just as you can't judge a home by its exterior, you can't judge a book by the cover. "So don't make judgments about anyone before the appointed time; wait until the Lord comes. He will bring our darkest secrets to light and will reveal our private motives. Then God will give to each one whatever praise is due." **1 Corinthians 4:5** When you have welcomed the Lord into your site to take full control, He will set you on a path to perfect everything on the inside of you. God sees any and all hidden agendas and motives of both man and woman's hearts. It is the difference between perfection without a purpose or passion and success without joy or lasting fulfillment. A home built to perfection without trials, modifications, or obstacles does not exist. But a home that is built and modified to perfection that is customized to meet all of your needs through your experience and understandings of

your needs can exist. Just remember that blueprints can

always be changed by the Master Builder to accommodate

changes in the environment and to adapt to different

challenges that come according to the area they are in.

Does your plan need to be able to overcome harsh weather

like hurricanes that require substances different from those

that need to withstand earthquakes? A home that is built to

withstand hurricanes will be built with concrete walls and not

mere drywall. It will also be reinforced with steel in the

framing as opposed to two by four wood framing. Homes

built in the middle of the water, on a mountain side, on sand or

on clay and rocks are all built with different considerations

and characteristics in mind. Sometimes it takes a certain type

of blueprint to weather certain storms that are destined to

come your way. Have you ever seen a home built around

many others that looked the same as all the others in a

neighborhood, yet when a storm hit that home was the only home still standing? The home may have showed little to no damage and seemed free from any of the distress of the past events that had just caused devastation all around it. When this happens, that home becomes the Glory of the owner, and also glorifies the Master Builder that orchestrated the plans for such a home. Everyone will want to know what the builder used to create such a strong and lasting design. Just as others will want to have their homes rebuilt with the same sterner stuff or use the master plans that were created for you. You were designed with a customized set of blueprints that can adapt, be modified, and tailor-made with advance secrets of uncommon wisdom to withstand any storm. **Proverbs 10:25,** "When the storms of life come, the wicked are whirled away, but the Godly stand firm forever." Sometimes your plans may appear to be just like everyone else, but the single most substantial thing you have that the others may not have is your faith and God's Favor, which are all you need. **Mathew 7:25,** "The rain came down, the streams rose, and the winds blow and beat against that house; yet it did not fall, because it had its foundation on the rock." We serve an awesome, all-knowing, loving God that is concerned about every detail in our plans as the Master Builder. Think about what you enjoy and truly desire and stop trying to design and plan on your own site, according to the limitations that only you put on yourself. Triumph over your mind and lean not to your own understanding. Do you really want to trust your own qualifications to design the master plans for the rest of your life? Just as you would call on a subcontractor for all those huge and insurmountable jobs that you are Not Qualified to do, stand where you are and ask God to provide you with a customized blueprint that has been commissioned just for you. Ask Him to provide you with all of the resources, finances, tools, and heart necessary to build your dream plan.

Jesus already negotiated your best contract and paid for it in full with His blood. It is only fair to honor the sacrifice He made us by living according to His decree for us that we would have the very thing that He died for us to have. In **John 10:10 Jesus says,** "The thief comes only to steal, kill and destroy; I have come that they may have life and have it abundantly." There will be people that will come against you at every pivotal point in your life. There will always be challenges before there is change. They will come to discourage you and attempt to deposit thoughts into your mind that you can't do something or you can't take any more than where you are at that very moment. Never accept defeat before asking God to come to you and deliver you from any of the issues you are dealing with. By doing this, you dishonor the very reason Jesus gave His life for you. **John 5:40,** "Yet you refuse to come to me to have life." I know some of you are saying I've got this, but can you think of someone else that doesn't? All He wants us to do is come to Him and ask Him

to custom build our plans and to save us according to His

unfailing Love! Then He wants us to walk in the anointing of

knowing that you are custom built by the Master Builder with

a purpose in mind. Every thought and every action that aligns

within the realm of what you are intended to do will empower

you to go a little farther the next time, to jump over the next

hurdle instead of running in to it. You will become wiser and

not weaker, steadfast in knowing that you can conquer and

achieve anything that you put your mind to achieve.

Be careful to give most of your attention to the things you

desire and not the things that you don't. You will become

more joyful thinking of constructive plans that will endure

anything and everything that comes your way. These plans

exist for each one of us and all you have to do is envision

those plans as already in stock for you to grab from the shelf.

He will provide you will all you need to start building right now.

Are You Ready For Your Home Inspection?

Now you know who the Master Builder is over your life,

and that you have a Paid-in-Full, All Expenses included, pre-

negotiated contract with the ability to acquire your custom-

built and tailor made plans. You also have been provided with

a 24/7 full-time, always available and eager to assist,

Developer Consultant. With all of these resources that God

has furnished us with, we are crazy not to take advantage of

doing a home inspection. Well, what is a home inspection? A

home inspection is when you take a visual look at the structure

and all aspects of your home to find items that are not

performing correctly or items that are unsafe which may pose

a problem in the future. If there is a problem, or a symptom of

a problem, the home inspector will include a written report

with the description of the problem and costs associated.

Sometimes, we need to do our own home inspection and

personal assessment to hone in on the aspects of our home and ourselves that is not pleasing to God or our future. Don't be intimidated by the level or magnitude of the issues or time that is necessary to effectively change or correct the deficiencies exposed during your inspection. Remain humble when you make a mistake, understanding that your need to change requires the maturity to know that you are not perfect. You are not to deny your strengths, but only to be honest about your weaknesses.

You have to ask yourself the hard questions like, "do your actions represent integrity, nobility, righteousness, goodness, meekness, and most of all, Love"! Are you easily angered and quick to respond in a negative manner before truly considering a more Godly approach? Oddly enough, I was recently reminded that to be Godly is not the same as being God-like. To be God-like means to show true love and patience in spite of the event at hand. Are you putting God in all of your decisions? In the decisions involving all of your personal, business, friends, family, associates and even those that you meet on the street? **Ephesians 4:2,** "Always be humble and gentle. Be patient with each other, making allowance for each other's faults because of your love."

Are you exercising self-control in your daily journey? Are you ever out of control and know it to be the case, but continue to make excuses for it? Is your attitude in check and your temper tamed? God wants us to exercise self-control and continue to be renewed in our minds and in our spirit. Sometimes your greatest challenge and yet simple instruction is to be still. As it says in **Psalm 46:10**, "Be still and know that I am God; I will be exalted among the nations, I will be exalted in the earth." Remember that it is written in **1 Peter 1:3**, "His divine power has given us everything we need for life and godliness through our knowledge of Him who called us by His own glory and goodness." These words mean that there are no excuses for our behavior because God has already given each of us the power to change inside and out. He has already fortified us with the Holy Spirit to enhance anything that we desire for the edification and glorifying of God. You have to be determined to take care of all of the iniquities and unwanted possessions of our home. He wants us to put off the old man as He says in Ephesians and put on the new man and be members one for another. We must exercise this commitment to change, because with it brings patience, endurance, and godliness given to us through the fruits of the spirit.

Are you doing things behind closed doors and know that you should make changes? I would gladly have loss here on earth for profits in heaven. When you assess what is on the inside of yourself, you must think of what your motives are and what it is that makes you a unique creature for God and not yourself. Clean up the dark spots and allow yourself to be held accountable by someone to let you know when you may not be on the road that leads to your ultimate place of perfection. You must first be accountable to yourself and truly be filled with thanks for who you are.

The fear of God is the first entrance to wisdom and understanding of these traits. **Acts 19:36,** "<u>Therefore, since these facts are undeniable, you ought to be quiet and not do anything reckless.</u>" We have the Developer/Consultant on call 24/7. We have been given carte-blanche to call on Him whenever we need to fix something about ourselves.

Are you being fair to everyone you come in contact with, not just your loved ones? Are you being fair and impartial to those who are in your work, on the phone, in your neighborhood, in your business, in stores, with customer service personnel, in your church, with people that help or assist you and wherever you go? Are you an embodiment of the grace and love that you have been afforded. **Luke 6:32,** "<u>and if ye love those loving you, what grace have ye? For</u>

also the sinful love those loving them." When we show grace or love to someone whom we feel doesn't deserve it, this is when God truly gets the glory. He will build in you a strong tower committed to defeat the labels placed inside of you that no one or anything will be able to tear you away from the glory of God, because He can take pleasure in that which He has made or restored.

Our inner assessment or home inspection should cause you to affect change and give refuge to new intentions and objectives. You have to get right from within and then your whole world will begin to reveal new attributes that you never knew you had. You become a better person and create a more peaceful environment for your construction site. It is your inside presence and not your outward appearance that gives you comfort, confidence, and an enthusiasm for living. Your outward appearance is only pleasing to others while you may be hurting or creating your own negative magnetism from within. **John 1:16,** "From His fullness, we all received grace

upon grace." Just as God does not argue with us and fight

with us, you have to assess your energy gage.

Are you constantly arguing and fighting with people? Do

you always feel like you need to get your point across? There

is a saying that goes, *be careful of arguing too long with a*

fool, lest you forget which one you are.

Are you living with joy and peace in your home? I call

silence a secret weapon. A useful tool when you are having a

terrible argument or disagreement is to pause for a moment in

the middle of the chaos. Watch and see what happens when

you pause. When the other person does not hear you

responding for at least five seconds when your next argument

occurs, you will notice that at first they will continue to argue;

then they will say things that may even justify your point of

view, if you are silent for long enough, without your fighting for it. This is an example of using the secret weapon of short silence to gain a little control.

Now, I will tell you a story that may at first seem hard to believe that it can reveal the true nature of a person's feelings about you. While you are doing your home inspection, you may want to inspect some of the pipelines to places that are supplying your water, heat, or energy. You may want to test out the integrity of the lines that are bringing all types of supply inside of you. Sometimes you may have to re-pipe, re-plumb, or re-wire where your lines have been compromised. One of my mentors told me, "You really want and need to know who you are bringing into your house."

I was in the middle of a big business transaction that was going to tie me to a group of individuals, and merge my business with their business. The amount that my partners were bringing to the table was approximately $40 million dollars and it involved a commodity. My mentor said that He did not trust the people we were going to bring forward and they would hold on to the money until the end of this test. I can say now that I was testing my water lines that were going to my house. My mentor told me to use the secret weapon that I had grown fond of using in small instances to reveal whether this business partner has good intentions or evil intentions. I could not imagine that this person would be any different than they had been for the last nine months of our relationship. My mentor told me I would not need longer than seven days to accomplish this test. I trust this person to not only bring out the best in me, but have my best interest at heart at all times.

He told me not to say anything to the guy for seven days. I knew this was going to be hard because I had been speaking to them in the morning and a few times throughout the day. We even had an internal common affection for the sunrise sky. All of my conversations with him and his wife were pleasant and we always seemed to get along and have a mutual affinity for the business we were building together. I had spoken to his partners and they all seemed to be a good fit. Nobody could have prepared me for what was about to happen over the next few days.

Day One. I received a phone call from the proposed partner and he was just calling to say "Hey" and wondered how I was doing. It was all the same to me. This was not out of the ordinary. However, I did not return the calls, which were only two the first day.

Day Two and Three. I received calls early in the morning, and even late at night. He said that he was a little surprised that he did not hear from me, but that he hoped all was well and to get back to him as soon as I could.

Day Four. I received a call from him that showed his frustration in the tone of his voice and in the tempered words he spoke. He said, "How can you take my calls and not call me back? This is unlike you. Call me to let me know what is going on. You need to call me if you still want to do this deal."

Day Five. I received a phone call and he told me that he knew that I was getting his calls and was not returning them. He was unsure if I was in the hospital or home, but he wanted to let me know something. He said, "If you don't call me by the end of the day, there will be some repercussions involved." I really wanted to call him and my mentor encouraged me to continue on that journey. He promised that it would all be worth the journey. Good or bad, the benefits would outweigh the torment of the task.

Day Six. Well right on schedule, I began to receive a deluge of phone calls from him and his partners. I had about twenty phone calls throughout the day. By night's end, they began to leave messages that were defamatory and offensive in nature. I felt hurt and I was truly disappointed at the tone and level of insults that had begun to surface. I called my mentor and told him about the instances and nature of the calls. He did not seem at all surprised and told me to continue through my last day. He said, "A snake will always reveal itself at some point, and I have found if you take away something that it wants, it will come out of the dark."

Day Seven. On this day, I pretty much had a glimpse of where this day was going to end up. I knew that this would be a very hard day, but my mentor told me to wait until 5pm before returning the call to the proposed business partner. The potential partner called and in his last comment stated, "I knew I should not have connected with you. I told them that getting this through a woman would not be a good idea. You have just shown me that you are not worth it and you have wasted all of my time. You are just a waste of time. If you think about crawling back to me at some point, just lose my number." He said I was a crook and a sheisty fake who should have never been trusted. Now some of you may feel like it was my fault, and may even feel like I deserved those comments because I made him wait. But ask yourself if you truly have admiration for someone, or you truly have confidence and trust in them, if you would feel like that after 7 days without contact? Would you condemn them without knowing if they were okay, without knowing if they had something that may have affected them in such a way that they were unable to get to you? Would you lose all caring or concern for them, and express such disdain and contemptuous emotions toward them? No, you would not, and the only reason that would happen is if you never had true feelings or positive intentions in the first place. Needless to say, I was hurt, disappointed, and felt betrayed. And at the same time, I felt like I was under attack.

Before the end of the day, I received a very strong *Cease and Desist* document from them.

I lost a financial backer, who had done some legal due diligence on the potential business partner and was very upset with me for even bringing him forward for funds from him. I called him on that day and wanted to explain myself, but he did not want to hear anything I was saying. I actually felt horrible and relieved at the same time. I felt like I had just been saved from a future with someone that I could not trust to have my best interest at heart at any time.

This may seem drastic, but I ask you to think about a situation in your life where you wished you would have known the true intentions of someone you thought had your best interest in mind, only to find out that it was a game or their intent to deceive you all along. There have been a few situations where the enemy was cunning and I never saw it coming. I thank God for this hard, yet useful tool that served me well in this regard.

So while you are doing your home inspection, you should take care to remove all of the other parts of your life, which include people that should not be in your life. Clean up and clean out your closets and create a space for you that will start to attract what you are putting out into the world. You have to challenge yourself to reach a higher level of peace from within your home and allow yourself the privilege of removing those that do not complement you or the life that you want to live.

When you are getting ready to have a conversation or an argument that you feel you are prepared to have, first start off knowing that you do not have to justify yourself to anyone other than God. Second, at the beginning of your conversation, ask yourself if the next words that are going to come out of your mouth are going to ultimately give God the glory and honor or give the enemy praise and pleasure. And third, constantly remember why you are having the conversation in the first place, always keeping the end result you hope to achieve in mind and not letting the journey take you so far off course that you never reach your intended destination. Always remember, everything that is good and perfect, God wants for you and diabolical forces always want the exact opposite. **Mathew 15:11,** "what goes into a man's mouth does not make him unclean, but what comes out of his mouth, that is what makes him unclean." If you think that the enemy is not using you through the words you speak, think again. People say things like "well at least, if I get it off my chest, I will feel better." That is all the trick of the enemy. There is nothing new under the sun. This is no different than that of any quick and short lived pleasure that causes you to have to endure something as a consequence that could last a lifetime. **James 3:6,** "The tongue also is a fire, a world of evil among the parts of the body. It corrupts the whole person, sets the whole course of his life on fire, and is itself set on fire by hell." You have to call on your Developer/Consultant to help you solve problems and not allow your irresponsible will to create problems. There is a prayer in **Ephesians 4:29** "Let no corrupt communication proceed out of your mouth, but that which is good to the use of edifying, that it may minister grace unto the hearers." This is a good word to speak over yourself and to declare effective communication over your life according to the will of God and His glorification. Wouldn't it be nice to be able to speak and know that the person to whom you are speaking receives every word that you are saying and it actually ministers to them?

Can you be trusted and do you have honor and loyalty? Do you gossip or engage in unhealthy conversations about people? **Proverbs 20:19**, "A gossip betrays confidence; so avoid a man who talks too much." These words tell us how we need to conduct ourselves. We have to remember to speak a little less and guard our speech. We must always be reminded that "All things work together for the good of those who love him, who have been called according to His purpose." **Romans 8:28**

When we do our home inspection and we find out those areas where we are lacking, we have to take time and care to resolve all the issues and trust that the Master Builder can fix it all. **Proverbs 18:21** "Death and life are in the power of the tongue; and they that love it shall eat the fruit thereof." Whatever needs you have at the moment, the answer is to be found in scripture and all we need to do is take the time to search for it and then own it from within. You can only pour out that which has been put inside of you. Surround yourself with positive people and information. Be ever so careful to feed yourself with the best and positive food you can. Stay with the nourishment from the source. Whatever you are feeling, whatever you are suffering from, and whatever you're hoping for, the Bible can address each and every item that is written on your home inspection list.

We also have a Developer / Consultant, "the Holy Spirit," to help us understand and put into practice our tools and methods. **John 4:2,** "You do not have, because you do not ask." We can clean up every aspect of our inspection list by just asking in faith. You have power that is unlimited beyond anything you could ever imagine when you learn that the first chapter of the Word, which He gave us for our instruction, gives each of us dominion over any and all things on earth. Every need that glorifies God, He has promised He will fix and align according to the plans He has for us. **Jeremiah 29:12,** "Then you will call upon me and come and pray to me, and I will listen to you." We can't be too lazy to do a full inspection on our own house right now.

What will give God the desire to choose you as His next construction site? But "if you pay attention to these laws and are careful to follow them, then the Lord your God will keep His covenant of Love with you, as He swore to your

<u>forefathers.</u>" **Deuteronomy 7:12**   We have to take care of ourselves and pay close attention to live as He has asked of us, and then all of His promises are ours, and He takes pleasure in knowing that you took your time to do your own home inspection and cared enough to address the issues that His son Jesus already paid for. And now He, *the Master Builder*, can trust you as His next construction site, worthy of His time and worthy of His personally qualified *Developer/ Consultant* in order to build a mansion for you. God wants you to give him the pleasure, the honor and the gratitude by perfecting your site with purpose. Your committed efforts glorify God by your beauty and the sacrifice it represents.

Assessing Your Site Location

One of the things that you must consider for a construction site is the costs and the prep work needed. We also would consider the infrastructure, the location, the foundation, and the quality of the site location. Remember, the cost of your site was Paid-in-Full when Jesus died. We realized that God was our Master Builder and He sees our site as prime real estate. Our location is key to the work we may have to do in His kingdom. If you live in the hood, a less desirable area, or have friends, co-workers, family members, or people that are around us that "need a little more Jesus," then He can use you for His glory. Think about Noah, whom God chose as one of His construction sites. God prepped him because of all of the corruption in the world; God saw him as Prime Real Estate and had him build an Ark in the middle of a dry land.

God tends to do the tasks that seem completely out of line with the logical will of man. He determines if your foundation needs a little more soil and also determines how He needs to prepare you with the proper infrastructure that is strong and resilient enough to preach good news to the poor, heal the hearts of the broken hearted, guard up the weak with His armor, and give freedom to those who are held captive in their own minds. He infuses the very foundation you have with the authority to command your location to be filled with all the resources you need to sustain your purpose. All of your provisions have been stored up and appointed by Him to stand strong at your request to carry you through the storms that will come. **Proverbs 10:25,** "When the storms of life come, the wicked are whirled away, but the Godly stand firm forever!" You may feel lost where you are, but your positioning is exactly where God wants you to be. Your positioning can be the main reason you were chosen as a vessel to be used in a dry land to bring water to the weak or weary. You are not only prime real estate, but you are a majestic person that God created with His purpose in mind. You are going to leave your footprints in the earth. Your imprint is to be left as a legacy through your inheritance from Jesus Christ. There are hidden treasures in each and every one of God's ordained children. As Joshua was instructed, we are also instructed that we should meditate on the Word and all of the life applications that are to be used for achieving a divine relationship with God and not man. **Joshua 1:8,** "This book of the law shall not depart from your mouth, but you shall meditate on it day and night so that you may be careful to do according to all that is written in it; for then you will make your way prosperous, and then you will have success." This is for your edification and perfecting of the power that resides inside you. You have the ability to adjust your location. Whether you are weak or just weakened by trials, your abilities are not revealed in the magnitude they exist until you have relinquished your will to His. Your personal desire to surrender full control and truly embody the love that only comes from God himself will

catapult you into a new dimension of awareness. All things

are possible for him that loves the Lord. You can achieve

better positioning by revoking anything that is not of God.

Get in your quiet space with the Lord, whether it is in your

car, a silent room in your home, a bench in the park or just a

quiet walk with God. If you need a location adjustment, you

can rely on God's omniscient ability to lead you to that place.

Asking him to position you daily to fulfill His desires of your

ordained future will keep you in the will of His kingdom.

There are many people that will come into your life that will

be able to teach you how to become in harmony with the

frequencies of God that allow your location to be anointed and

powerful. We have a choice daily to change our physical

location, mental location or level, and spiritual location or

level of connection with the Holy Spirit. When you ignore

the distractions of your world and give God the opportunity to communicate HIS desires for your life, you will begin to notice a whole new world that does not exist to the person without the consistent relationship of communicating with God, and not just to God. In **Genesis 28:15** the Lord says "I am with you and will watch over you wherever you go, and I will bring you back to this land. I will not leave you until I have done what I have promised you." Your current location may be chosen and appointed as Prime Real Estate for God. Take a few quiet moments to find out how to move into perfect alignment with the will of God. This is a worthwhile assignment for your assurance and true satisfaction with the freedom you have to express yourself, knowing that you are exactly where you are supposed to be. Having a consistent time when you communicate with God will change your direction, generate and cultivate your vision, and give reason to your intuitive nature that gives you new or continued focus and provides energy for your journey.

Honor Your Site With Acceptance

Once you have accepted that the Master Developer has

chosen your site, you should get excited. When God starts

working in you, your journey becomes part of the

development He needs for you to obtain. Your life obstacles

become your main anchors for the foundation He wants to

infuse in you for your steadfastness. When you have begun to

honor what He is doing within you, your faith gets stronger,

and your will gets unshakable, and your walk becomes straight

and focused. After He has worked with you and you have

accepted His direction, you will be able to see that changes are

being orchestrated for your mansion to be built right where

you stand. You have to stay focused on the end result of what

God is doing within you. I suggest you keep a journal to write

the vision that you see for yourself through the eyes of God

and not man. I want you to envision and then write your

vision plain. In **Habakkuk 2:2,** God himself says, "Write down the vision and make it plain upon tablets that He may run that reads it." Write it from the viewpoint of how God sees your life and all of the good and perfect designs He has for you. He instructs us to do this when you are in a place of need and want Him to reveal His direction for you. Resist the urge to write from your own limited perspective and remember to remain in the unlimited nature of where God can and is leading you. You have accepted that you have a prime location or are moving to that place, so identify with the most perfect location you can imagine.

Understand that you will go through pressures and have to call in your Consultant from time to time. Your growth will come in the form of some challenges. Challenges bring forth change with respect and authority over a situation and provide more wisdom and understanding in the responsibility you have for God and the people He wants you to serve. Be open-minded and resist all temptation to control everything that you are led to do or say. Relinquish your control and submit yourself humbly before God. Your honor and obedience to His word will keep you in the perfect will of God, but the desires of those that don't want you to succeed will come against you at your pivotal point of change. Remember to keep Him in the middle of all of your thoughts, actions, movements, and decisions.

When you wake up in the morning, you should spend at least 5, 10, or 30 minutes with God and know that He will direct your paths. If you are already doing this, then you are ahead of most in having a daily consistent prayer life with God, which includes Pastors and Officiates in ministry. During your commune, ask for your paths to be shod with the Armor of God. **Ephesians 6:15** "and having shod your feet with the preparation of the Gospel of Peace; Above all, taking the shield of faith, wherewith ye shall be able to quench all the fiery darts of the wicked". God can disperse His

administrative angels ahead of you to work on your behalf.

When you prepare for sleep, spend time with God as well

and allow Him to be in your last thoughts before you go to

bed. God and His Holy Spirit work on you and in you while

you are sleeping. When you are in your darkest times, you

have to know that He will never leave you nor forsake you.

Even when you think He is not there for you, and you think

you are all alone, you have to trust in the omniscience of God.

Your honor to God will bring Him to your rescue where you

don't have to see Him instead; your faith becomes your seed

to bring forth the power of God to change your mindset to a

place of purpose through whatever trials come. You have to

change through your challenges. Once your mindset and your

acceptance have allowed God to work on you, He will begin

to build the Greatest Structure of You. Sometimes you have

to give up false friends, and move from forgiveness to

forgetfulness, which is all God-ordained. You have to leave

some situations that you know are not based on God's call on

your life. He does not want you to allow everyone to walk in

to the hallways of your life or your heart. God will nudge you

with gentle urges that will still your spirit and replenish your

soul with new found poise in situations where you had none.

He will also fill your spirit with passion and a zest for life

itself. He has to build you up and strengthen you to be able to

handle transgression that comes for you in your weakest

moments. He will put a little wisdom on the inside of you to

deal with the obstacles, people, and trials that will come your

way. When you are built with the sterner stuff that God

himself has placed within the weavings of your heart, you will

operate from a place of peace with your decisions and the

stamina that parallels the roots of an oak tree. Your

foundation will be strong and able to endure all that comes,

with a firm acceptance of the lesson behind the events in your life. Your vision will become clear and your confidence will take you into the finest places you are only able to enter based on favor that permits you to fill your mansion with extraordinary, ordained products.

Once you have been elevated to a level that allows you to walk in your authority and power, your attitude will begin to reflect your transformation and ultimately change your latitude for growth. When God is working in you, your depth and perception become greater and more defined. Obstacles and situations become clearer and uncommon courage is garnered without much effort. You have to complete this honor by asking Him to bring your pathways into light with His directives for you.

When this begins to happen in the flow and current that God orchestrates, the enemy will try to get you off the path. **2 Timothy 3:12,** "In fact, everyone who wants to live a godly life in Christ Jesus will be persecuted." Your inner desires will become your biggest challenges. When God's desire for you, begins to align with your internal thinking and your belief system, you will feel more empowered and strengthened by your purpose. He wants to be your Developer and build you with the power to affect life itself to His glory. When God is finished building your thoughts and inner power, He will send those to you to test your growth for your personal confirmation and edification of who you are becoming.

When you come to greater levels of living, your trials will grow with the level of growth. If you have ever been through a trial, the next time the same trial comes, you are able to give meaning to the past pain for a purpose of self-assurance based on your past victories and overcoming results. God will bring someone else to you that needs an encouraging word or comforted confidence that you can provide through your experiences that enable God to get the Glory. It is in these victories and overcoming moments that tenacity is derived and testimonies for the disheartened or discouraged are developed.

God uses your pain and heartache for an ultimate purpose.

Your journey is always for God's final masterpiece. Your

destination is based on your defining qualities, characteristics,

and strengths. And your success and growth in life is

measured by the things you are willing to ignore. When you

don't put your deadbolt on the new home that God is building

for you, you do not honor the trust He has put in you that you

will honor all that He has done inside of you. He wants you to

guard over all that you are fighting to achieve and accomplish.

God wants to work through you to fulfill His will.

It matters how much time you allow yourself to become

subjected to those who you know should not be in your life,

and the conversations and decisions you make because they

please others and do not serve you. When you are on track to

have all you need, sometimes the enemy will come in the form

of a friend with an opportunity or event that will take you off focus of the path you are on. Be careful to make decisions that will serve God's plan for your life first and not that of someone else. The enemy will try to throw you off the mark by whatever means he can find. Your friends or associates may not even know that they are being used. Ultimately, your decisions count and may delay or even dismiss a success milestone predicated by your judgments in life. We all have to learn how to say no to people that we care about and know that it is in your best interest to stay on a God given journey than any opportunity that man brings. A missed opportunity is an opportunity that just went on to the next willing participant.

You will know when God is working through you, because you will be able to serve others through your walk. You may even have been fed at a time when you were hungry and hunger for someone will be abolished. You may have had a broken heart that God has mended and the broken hearted person will be comforted by your will and testimony of love.

God wants us to bring love to those that feel lost and He says greater is He that is in you, than he that is in the world.

Accepting His development in you will mean you will begin to experience the trials of others to listen, encourage, uplift, cultivate, empower, inspire, serve, promote, and ultimately and honorably bring peace to the life of someone through the Power of Christ's salvation and sacrifice. It ultimately becomes a sacrifice for you that can come out of the abundance of the gifts that God has given you and the fruits of the Spirit. He needs you to serve His people and to know that He can trust you to carry out His good and perfect will.

The Landscape

When God decides to alter or enhance your landscape, He will allow plants to grow with amazing color and long life in your yard that will attract people to stop and speak to you or come in and visit with you. He will begin to enlarge your territory for him by the appearance and presence that your outer surroundings illuminate. When He develops and plans out your plot and begins to change the landscape on the outside to compliment the seeds that He planted inside your soil, the flowers begin to bloom in full color, the grass thickens, and your walkway becomes clearly defined and concise. In **Deuteronomy 8:11,** "Be careful that you do not forget the Lord your God, failing to observe His commands, His laws and His decrees that I am giving you this day." You are going to have to water the flowers once they bloom with the continuous Word of God. You will have to cut the grass to keep it from overtaking the flowers and growing beyond the design that has been planned. Just as God has designed us for His glory, He continues to prune and care for our directions and purpose, just as you will do the same for yourself. He is leading you by His example so that you will be an example that will draw others to Him by your success and attractiveness. You may have to remove some dry spots or take out some sections that are not growing properly and replace the challenged areas with new sod or plug in fresh soil and fertilizer. Your reading of His word will continue to work on any of the iniquities that are within you that need to be pulled out. God's Word becomes fertilizer to keep the grass green and strong and appearing flawless in the site of others. You will never be completely without sin, but your spiritual appearance will be protected by God's ability to restore and replenish you with water and Word whenever necessary. You may have to pull weeds from the walkway to your new home. Weeds continue to grow and they appear to come out of nowhere and in places you feel they could not grow. Just remember that sometimes you have to weed out to see clearly the beauty that lies within. There will always be weeds that will come and try to divert the beauty that God has given you. Your constant care and elimination of weeds in your life are just a part of the reminder that there is something that your beauty has that the enemy wants to steal and it's your job to defeat and keep your weed-be-gone Bible around to diffuse the enemy each time they come. Never let them get so overgrown that they come into the crevices of your house. Continue to stay alert and on guard, separating the weeds from the flowers, identifying and discerning malicious foliage that is out of place and constantly giving love and attention to your landscape. Others may see some of your weaknesses, but your desire and endearing capacity to never let them overtake you because of your diligent attention and work to keep your home in its proper vision will deter the enemy from feeling like you are an easy target.

Your landscape will be customized to fit your personality and complement your home with accents and features that will allow you to shine.

Sometimes Your Site Location Has To Change

When you are chosen by the Master Builder and you begin to experience the power of God changing within you, you have to accept that your current location may change. When the Master Builder begins to pour into your life, your design and plans may not fit your current soil or surface. He may have to place you on richer ground or on the contrary, even broken ground to complete the strength of the foundation needed for your journey. You have to make sure that the home you want to have built is not being developed in a place you know is not the best fit for you. You have to be willing to move according to your design. Sometimes you need to move in order for God to be able to use your house as a display and anchor for His work through you. When you allow His Developer Consultant to guide you and place you in the path of His blessings, you can move by your faith and not by your might. You will begin to feel and experience a supernatural pull or tug on your heart that goes beyond explanation. God will help you to accomplish a move that may seem unfathomable or impossible. When you trust him for your future and purpose, He will begin to reveal where and which direction you need to be. **Ezekiel 37:14,** "I will put my Spirit in you and you will live, and I will settle you in your own land. Then you will know that I the LORD have spoken, and I have done it, declares the LORD."

When you experience a mighty move of God in your life, you have to have the faith that the decisions you are led to make will bring forth life to your heart, mind and your body. When you have a location change, it can mean the difference between life and death, depression and joy, ailments and healing, failures and accomplishments, restoration and destruction, enduring and flourishing, or darkness and light. In the right position, God can firmly implement the plans He has for you. You have blockers in your life that will come around you and try to place inside of you thoughts that are

destructive and discouraging. Confusion comes when there is

no understanding of your purpose. It is absolutely detrimental

to your purpose that you move to a place conducive to

receiving and developing a true relationship with God. Each

one of us has a seed that has been planted inside. More

sunlight, a warmer climate, or just a slight shift in the direction

you are facing may be all that is needed for God to take you

from an impeded or stunted position to a flourishing, thriving

life full of the abundance and success. You have to place

yourself in a surrounding that is going to feed your spirit with

the nourishment that is from God and His love alone, and

allow others that have your best interest in mind to pour into

your life. When you are presented with a location change,

often your resistance is a sign that there is something greater

available that you have to break into or break out of. If you

have a location change, remember as He says in **Genesis 46:3**

"I am God, the God of your father," he said. "Do not be afraid to go down to Egypt, for I will make you into a great nation there." Wherever your Egypt is God will be there. There is a place that will allow you to feel as if you are riding a huge wave or current, taking you without effort to a place where you become more creative and inspired to do whatever is necessary to face the challenges you have.

Are you in a place where there is chaos or that is life threatening and you know this is not where He wants you to be? Is your area too loud or even too messy? Are your surroundings cluttered with things that will inhibit you from praise and comfortable communication when you need to be in His presence? If any of this is true for your current home site, you may need a location change. Whether the change is physical or mental, be encouraged that the fight for it is worth it. The end result will be stress-free, but the journey may undoubtedly cause you to be tested.

We often say that your faith is not truly revealed until it is truly put to the test and it is needed. If you have never been in a chaotic environment without love, understanding, and support, then you won't be able to truly appreciate the depth of gratitude you will have when it is achieved. When you move to or abide in the perfect location where God can use you, you will be filled with anticipation and emphatic feelings that influence others to participate in assisting you in the fulfillment of your dreams and aspirations. Others will participate in your vision with a pure and unconditional desire and enthusiasm to help you. Greatness will never be achieved alone; and "Nothing great was ever achieved without enthusiasm." (Ralph Waldo Emerson)

Your Mansion Is Paid-In-Full.

Ephesians 3:20, "<u>Now unto him who is able to do immeasurably more than all we ask or imagine, according to His power that is at work within us.</u>" I want you to imagine God building in you a mansion right where you stand, Paid-in-Full with the blood of Jesus Christ. Every debt, every need, and every desire that you would have for your life is Paid-in-Full.

Every aspect of your life is filled with purpose and refined with flawless and unconditional love. Every physical adjustment has been restored to better than you ever imagined possible. Receive the wisdom and understanding that God's greatest gift and request for and from you is love and compassion. Receive these thoughts and partake in your vision as if you were already granted a lamp with three wishes to pursue. If you practice these thoughts and put them out into the universe that God gave you dominion over, then you have to believe what you are obligated to honor as your divine revelation according to His power that is at work within you.

Imagine being able to see yourself in the mirror and truly loving and appreciating the person you are from the crown of your head to the tips of your toes, truly being built up with all the love, patience, wisdom, and strength within your walls to conquer anything that comes your way including death itself! Where there is true understanding, there is power to overcome all; no matter what trials you have caused, spiteful things you have done, dreams you have stolen, or even hatred you may have promoted. We serve a God that will forgive all of your faults. He is always standing, waiting, willing, ready and able to give you a fresh start for him. **1 John 2:1,** "My dear children, I write this to you so that you will not sin. But if anybody does sin, we have one who speaks to the Father in our defense – Jesus Christ, the righteous one."

I want you to sit right now and imagine yourself in a place where all your sins have been forgiven and washed away. Envision all of your issues being carried away farther and farther out into an ocean with every wave and current that pulls them to a point where you can't see them anymore. Any and all of your concerns are being washed out to sea and you are left free from even the glimpse of any of the negative concerns you once had. If you will practice this vision daily, for at least 30 consecutive days, you will begin to have less and less of your concerns remain in your shore from day to day that needs to be washed away. Declare that you have no insecurities and your heart is full of the unspeakable joy that comes from the Father alone.

Imagine being strong enough to walk away from trouble, and people that have hurt or betrayed you. Imagine being able to walk toward the enemies you were once fearful of with the courage and confidence to conquer them with words and wisdom from God. **Mathew 10:19, 20** "But when they arrest you, do not worry about what to say or how to say it. At that time you will be given what to say, for it will not be you speaking, but the Spirit of your Father speaking through you." You have a Father who is willing to sit at the Stern of your ship and guide you through the tumultuous conversations that may intimidate you, knowing as it says in **Luke 12:12**, "for the Holy Spirit will teach you at that time what you should say." Imagine having faith strong enough to conquer the enemies' strongholds on you. Imagine not letting anger overtake you, but having the discipline to never react to a situation but having the power and consciousness to pause whenever you need to, and bring yourself and your mental spirit back to a place of positive emotion. Imagine being able to say no to and walk away from anyone you know who is only trying to take advantage of you and being able to trust God to deal with them in His appointed time. Knowing that

He will, and remembering His goodness through your broken chains, mountains crossed and immeasurable wisdom that comes exactly when you need it. Controlling people and destructive thoughts are far from you. **Isaiah 40:29,** "He gives strength to the weak and increases the power of the weak."

Imagine being able to forgive those that have come against you or wronged you in some way, to be able to forgive those that have stolen from you. You will have the ability to operate in a Spirit of Joy when you are in the presence of someone who once made you fearful or angry. Imagine the Spirit of God residing in you and your site so strongly that you are attracting all the resources of God that are necessary to fulfill the desires of your heart. Every ailment you have endured is healed and every sickness is cured with your faith and anointing. Deceitful people and all people that do not have your best interests in mind will be revealed and consequently removed before your eyes, without conflict or confrontation.

You are finally free from all the restrictions that you put on yourself and are only limited by your own belief system. You finally trust God in all aspects of your life, trusting all the promises He left in His Word.

Well you have the right and assurance now that all of this IS yours for the asking; all you have to do is seek and you will find all the treasures that are hidden inside of you. Your understanding of the principles that are laid out for your life and your mansion is crucial and inevitably built right where you stand, strong and resolute with unyielding strength to overcome being broken. **Psalm 100:5,** "For the Lord your God is good and His love endures forever; His faithfulness continues through all generations." And that includes you and me!

Your mansion is ready and you are ready to let go of the past and be diligent over your new life. God loved us enough to renew our minds and you get to choose right now to accept your freedom from this world's limitations and any insecurity you may have had. It is up to you to imagine yourself with the gentleness and agility to astound the world with your Light. Splendid is the mansion that is built by fire, faith, and a firm foundation with all the wisdom of the Holy Spirit, the power of the blood behind you, and the characteristics of Jesus inside of you. **Psalm 18:2,** "I have told you these things, so that in me you may have peace. In this world, you will have trouble, but take heart! I have overcome the world." You have the protection promised to you for peace of mind. **Philippians 4:13,** "I can do all things through Him who gives me strength. For the Lord is my rock, my fortress and my deliverer; my God is my rock, in whom I take refuge. He is my shield and the horn of my salvation, my stronghold."

Remember your mansion is only established with the belief you have in your *Master Builder* and your decree to follow the principles and instructions planned by your blueprint. Trust your Master Builder, inquire and consult with your Developer, and thank Jesus for making the ultimate sacrifice for your mansion that is PAID-IN-FULL! You must live your Best, Blessed, and Bountiful Life right now, trusting God, and believing that everything I have said is true. At the age of 18 I created this quote that has remained an inspiring and truthful word of encouragement for me and others. *"**Better than your best is when your best gets blessed.**"* You are appointed and chosen, given supreme power and dominion over all the earth and all that dwells within it, to Live and not Die, allow God to create a custom built mansion for you! Give Him praises for what He is doing in you!

Your Insurance and Home Warranty
Protection Plan

You have been given a mansion, built with the Holy Spirit

as your Developer and orchestrated by the Master Builder. I

would be remised if I did not tell you about your Insurance

Plan and how to maintain your Magnificent Gift. You are not

only afforded with the mansion, but as Jesus has Paid-In-Full

for your mansion, so has He paid for your top of the line

Insurance Plan and your Home Warranty was put in place to

give you a complete understanding of all that is required to

maintain your home with the highest of excellence. He also

left us with His word. The Bible and all that is within it can

be looked at as your insurance plan that includes your home

warranty protection plan. You are not only insured, but

assured in the Word of God. Every kind of strife or situation

that you will endure can be found in the Bible. There are

many instructions and commandments to live by. One thing

you must remember is that we are charged to bring people into the Kingdom and we must maintain the policy that is put in place, or at any moment it could be taken away from the jealous God that we serve.

Deuteronomy 8, "Be careful to follow every command I am giving you today, so that you may live and increase and may enter and possess the land that the Lord promised on oath to your forefathers. Remember how the Lord your God led you all the way in the desert these forty years; to humble you and to test you in order to know what was in your heart, whether or not you would keep His commands. He humbled you, causing you to hunger and then feeding you with manna, which neither you nor your fathers had known, to teach you that man does not live on bread alone but on every word that comes from the mouth of the Lord. Your clothes did not wear out and your feet did not swell during these forty years. Know then in your heart as a man disciplines his son, so the Lord your God disciplines you. Observe the commands of the Lord your God, walking in His ways and revering him. For the

Lord your God is bringing you into a good land ---a land with

streams and pools of water, with springs flowing in the valleys

and hills; a land with wheat and barley, vines and fig trees,

pomegranates, olive oil and honey, a land where bread will not

be scarce and you will lack nothing; a land where the rocks are

iron and you can dig copper out of the hills. When you have

eaten and are satisfied, praise the Lord your God for the good

land He has given you. Be careful that you do not forget the

Lord your God, failing to observe His commands, His laws

and His decrees that I am giving you this day. Otherwise,

when you eat and are satisfied, when you build fine houses

and settle down, and when your herds and flocks grow large

and your silver and gold increase and all you have is

multiplied, then your heart will become proud and you will

forget the Lord your God, who brought you out of Egypt, out

of the land of slavery. He led you through the vast and

dreadful desert, that thirsty and waterless land, with its venomous snakes and scorpions. He brought you water out of hard rock. He gave you manna to eat in the desert, something your fathers had never known, to humble and to test you so that in the end it might go well with you. You may say to yourself, "My power and the strength of my hands have produced this wealth for me." But remember the Lord your God, for it is He who gives you the ability to produce wealth, and so confirms His covenant, which He swore to your forefathers as it is today.

If you ever forget the Lord your God and follow other Gods and worship and bow down to them, I testify against you today that you will surely be destroyed. Like the nations the Lord destroyed for not obeying the Lord your God."

I leave you with one of the most important chapters that I was told to read at a time in my life when I felt as if I was about to achieve all that God has pre-ordained for me. The individual who told me that the Lord himself commanded him to have me read this did not know that three days earlier I had just turned 40 years old. I was in the space of seeing myself as being fine, fit, and forty, fortified with a strong foundation of faith and being reminded not to forget the Lords Goodness and all that He has done for me. When I spoke those words over my life, they don't represent man's meager definition, but the confidence and true authority that represent the fact that I can truly say, "I Love Me Today." I am commissioned to provide the same word of knowledge and wisdom to all of you. Don't doubt God!

Our insurance plan gives us the vision and instruction to live according to His word. We can't let our circumstances dictate our joy. We can find joy in knowing that He will bring us through, triumphant and victorious. However, it is our mandate that we always remember to keep God as the *Master Builder*, the Holy Spirit as our *Developer/Consultant*, and

Jesus Christ as *Architect and Paymaster* who approved our mansion as Paid-In-Full in the forefront of our lives. May God continue to bless and keep us all in the covenant of His Word and in His Good and Perfect Will.

My Prayer

LORD, I THANK YOU FOR INSPIRING ME TO SHARE THE VISION THAT YOU HAVE GIVEN ME TO POUR OUT TO OTHERS THAT WHICH YOU HAVE POURED IN TO ME, AND THE WISDOM TO SHARE YOUR WORDS OF COMFORT, AND LOVE WITH AS MANY PEOPLE THAT ARE WILLING TO LISTEN. MAY YOUR PEOPLE ON EARTH AND EVERYONE WHO READS THIS BOOK BE INSPIRED, MOTIVATED AND EMPOWERED BY YOUR WORD. MAY THE WORDS THAT I SPEAK THROUGH THIS BOOK BRING LIFE TO THE WEARY AND BE FRUIT FOR YOUR PEOPLE ON EARTH. AMEN *SB*

<u>Bible Supportive Chapters and</u>
<u>Verses for Study</u>

Bible Chapter	*Supporting Scriptures*
Proverbs 3:5, 6	"Trust in the Lord with all your heart and lean not to your own understanding; acknowledge Him, and He will make all your paths straight."
Psalm 40:4	"Blessed is the man who makes the Lord his trust."
Luke 6:48	"he is like a man building a house, which is dug down deep and laid the foundation on rock. When a flood came, the torrent struck that house, but could not shake it because it was well built."
Isaiah 61:1	"The spirit of the Lord is on me, because the Lord has appointed me to preach good news to the poor. He has sent me to bind up the brokenhearted, to proclaim freedom for the captives and release from darkness for the prisoners".
Revelations 4:11	"You created everything, and it is for your pleasure that they exist and were created."
Psalm 149:4	"The Lord takes pleasure in his people."
Jeremiah 29:11	"For I know the plans I have for you," declares the Lord, "plans to prosper you and not to harm you, plans to give you hope and a future."
Proverbs 3:5,6	"Trust in the Lord with all your heart and lean not to your own understanding; acknowledge him, and he will make all your paths straight."
Psalm 40:4	"Blessed is the man who makes the Lord his trust."

Bible Chapter	*Supporting Scriptures*
John 4:16,17	"And I will ask the Father and he will give you another Counselor to be with you forever – the Spirit of truth. The world cannot accept him nor knows him. But you know him, for he lives with you and will be in you."
1 Corinthians 2:12	"For we have not received the Spirit of the World but the Spirit who is from God, that we may understand what God has freely given us."
Psalm 127:1	"Unless the Lord builds the house, its builder's labor in vain. Unless the Lord watches over the city, the watchmen stand guard in vain.."
Isaiah 43:1	"Fear Not, for I have redeemed you; I have summoned you by name; you are mine!"
1Peter 2:9	"But you are a chosen people, a royal priesthood, a Holy nation, a people belonging to God, that you may declare the praises of him who called you out of darkness into His wonderful light!"
Psalm 147:5	"How great is our Lord! His power is absolute! His understanding is beyond comprehension.."
2 Corinthians 12:9	"But he said to me, my grace is sufficient for you, for may power is made perfect in weakness. Therefore I will boast all the more gladly about my weaknesses, so that Christ's power may rest on me."
Corinthians 16:13	"Be on your guard; stand firm in the faith, be men of courage; be strong."
Joshua 10:25	And Joshua said unto them, "Fear not, nor be dismayed, be strong and of good courage: for thus shall the Lord do to all your enemies against whom you fight."
1 Peter 4:12	"Therefore let those who suffer according to God's will entrust their souls to a faithful Creator while doing good."

Bible Chapter	*Supporting Scriptures*
Jeremiah 30:17	"But I will restore you to health and heal your wounds, declares the Lord, because you are called an outcast, Zion for whom no one cares."
Psalm 119:71	"It was good for me to be afflicted, that I might learn thy decrees."
Psalm 54:4	"Surely God is my help; the Lord is the one who sustains me!"
Psalm 51:12	"restore to me the joy of your salvation and grant me a willing spirit, to sustain me"
2Corinthians 1:8	"We do not want you to be uninformed, brothers, about the hardships we suffered in the province of Asia. We were under great pressure for beyond our ability to endure, so that we despaired even of life!"
Psalm 73:26	"My flesh and my heart may fail, but God is the strength of my heart and my portion forever!"
Psalm 69:4	"Those who hate me without reason, outnumber the hairs on my head; many are my enemies without cause; those who seek to destroy me. I am forced to restore what I did not steal."
John 4:4	"Verily, verily, I say unto you, He that believeth on me, the works that I do shall he do also; and greater works than these shall he do; because I go unto my Father."
Psalm 25:17	"The troubles of my heart have multiplied; free me from my anguish."
Hebrews 6:10	"God is not unjust; he will not forget your work and the love you have shown him as you have helped his people and continue to help them."
John 14:2	"In my Father's house are many mansions: if it were not so, I would have told you. I go to prepare a place for you."

Bible Chapter	*Supporting Scriptures*
2 Chronicles 24:12	"The King hired subcontractors like masons and carpenters to restore the Lord's temple that specialized in bronze and iron to repair the temple."
Psalm 119:116	Lord, "sustain me as you promised that I may live. Do not let my hope be crushed!
2 Samuel 22:33	"God is my strong refuge and has made my way blameless."
Psalm 31:3	"Since you are my rock and my fortress, for the sake of your name, lead me and guide me."
Psalm 126:5	"Those who sow in tears will reap with songs of joy."
Psalm 71:8	"My mouth is filled with your praise, declaring your splendor all day long!"
Galatians 6:8	"The one who sows to please his sinful nature, from that nature will reap destruction; the one who sows to please the Spirit, from the Spirit will reap eternal life."
Hosea 10:13	"But you have planted wickedness, you have reaped evil, you have eaten the fruit of deception. Because you have depended on your own strength and on your many warriors,--"
Ephesians 3:20	"Now unto him that is able to do exceeding abundantly above all that we ask or think, according to the power that works within us."
1 Kings 3:13	"Moreover, I will give you what you have not asked for—both riches and honor –so that in your lifetime you will have no equal among Kings."
Colossians 4:12	"He is always wrestling in prayer for you, that you may stand firm in all the Will of God, mature and fully assured."
James 1:4	"for when your endurance is fully developed, you will be perfect and complete lacking in nothing".

Bible Chapter	*Supporting Scriptures*
Romans 15:32	"Then, by the will of God, I will be able to come to you with a joyful heart, and we will be an encouragement to each other."
1 Corinthians 4:5	"So don't make judgments about anyone before the appointed time; wait until the Lord comes. He will bring our darkest secrets to light and will reveal our private motives. Then God will give to each one whatever praise is due."
Proverbs 10:25	"When the storms of life come, the wicked are whirled away, but the Godly stand firm forever."
Mathew 7:25	"The rain came down, the streams rose, and the winds blow and beat against that house; yet it did not fall, because it had its foundation on the rock."
John 10:10	"The thief comes only to steal, kill and destroy; I have come that they may have life and have it abundantly."
John 5:40	"Yet you refuse to come to me to have life."
Ephesians 4:2	"Always be humble and gentle. Be patient with each other, making allowance for each ones others faults because of your love."
Psalm 46:10	"Be still and know that I am God; I will be exalted among the nations, I will be exalted in the earth."
1 Peter 1:3	"His divine power has given us everything we need for life and godliness through our knowledge of him who called us by His own glory and goodness."
Acts 19:36	"Therefore, since these facts are undeniable, you ought to be quiet and not do anything reckless."
Luke 6:32	"and if ye love those loving you, what grace have ye? For also the sinful love those loving them."
John 1:16	"From his fullness, we all received grace upon grace."

Bible Chapter	Supporting Scriptures
Mathew 15:11	"what goes into a man's mouth does not make him unclean, but what comes out of his mouth, that is what makes him unclean".
James 3:6	"The tongue also is a fire, a world of evil among the parts of the body. It corrupts the whole person, sets the whole course of his life on fire, and is itself set on fire by hell."
Ephesians 4:29	"Let no corrupt communication proceed out of your mouth, but that which is good to the use of edifying, that it may minister grace unto the hearers."
Proverbs 20:19	A gossip betrays confidence; so avoid a man who talks too much."
Romans 8:28	"All things work together for the good of those who love him, who have been called according to his purpose."
Proverbs 18:21	"Death and life are in the power of the tongue; and they that love it shall eat the fruit thereof."
John 4:2	"You do not have, because you do not ask."
Jeremiah 29:12	"Then you will call upon me and come and pray to me, and I will listen to you."
Deuteronomy 7:12	"if you pay attention to these laws and are careful to follow them, then the Lord your God will keep his covenant of Love with you, as he swore to your forefathers."
Proverbs 10:25	"When the storms of life come, the wicked are whirled away, but the Godly stand firm forever!"
Joshua 1:8	"This book of the law shall not depart from your mouth, but you shall meditate on it day and night so that you may be careful to do according to all that is written in it; for then you will make your way prosperous, and then you will have success."

Bible Chapter	*Supporting Scriptures*
Habakkuk 2:2	"Write down the vision, and make it plain upon tablets, that he may run that reads it."
Genesis 28:15	I am with you and will watch over you wherever you go, and I will bring you back to this land. I will not leave you until I have done what I have promised you."
2 Timothy 3:12	"In fact, everyone who wants to live a godly life in Christ Jesus will be persecuted,"
Deuteronomy 8:11	"Be careful that you do not forget the Lord your God, failing to observe his commands, his laws and his decrees that I am giving you this day."
Ezekiel 37:14	"I will put my Spirit in you and you will live, and I will settle you in your own land. Then you will know that I the LORD have spoken, and I have done it, declares the LORD.'"
Genesis 46:3	"I am God, the God of your father," he said. "Do not be afraid to go down to Egypt, for I will make you into a great nation there."
Ephesians 3:20	"Now unto him who is able to do immeasurably more than all we ask or imagine, according to his power that is at work within us."
1 John 2:1	"My dear children, I write this to you so that you will not sin. But if anybody does sin, we have one who speaks to the Father in our defense – Jesus Christ the righteous one."
Mathew 10:19,20	"But when they arrest you, do not worry about what to say or how to say it. At that time you will be given what to say, for it will not be you speaking, but the Spirit of your Father speaking through you."
Luke 12:12	"for the Holy Spirit will teach you at that time what you should say."

Bible Chapter	_Supporting Scriptures_
Isaiah 40:29	"He gives strength to the weak and increases the power of the weak."
Psalm 100:5	"For the Lord your God is good and his love endures forever; his faithfulness continues through all generations."
Psalm 18:2	"I have told you these things, so that in me you may have peace. In this world you will have trouble, but take heart! I have overcome the world."
Philippians 4:13	"I can do all things through him who gives me strength. For the Lord is my rock, my fortress and my deliverer; my God is my rock, in whom I take refuge. He is my shield and the horn of my salvation, my stronghold."
Deuteronomy 8	"Be careful to follow every command I am giving you today, so that; you may live and increase and may enter and possess the land that the Lord promised on oath to your forefathers. Remember how the Lord your God led you all the way in the desert these forty years, to humble you and to test you in order to know what was in your heart, whether or not you would keep his commands. He humbled you, causing you to hunger and then feeding you with manna, which neither you nor your fathers had known, to teach you that man does not live on bread alone but on every word that comes from the mouth of the Lord. Your clothes did not wear out and your feet did not swell during these forty years. Know then in your heart as a man disciplines his son, so the Lord your God disciplines you. Observe the commands of the Lord your God, walking in his ways and revering him. For the Lord your God is bringing you into a good land ---a land with streams and pools of water, with springs flowing in the valleys and hills; a land with wheat and barley, vines and fig trees, pomegranates, olive oil and honey, a land where bread will not be scarce and you will lack nothing; a land where the rocks are iron and you can dig copper out of the hills. When you have

	Cont'd – Deuteronomy 8
	eaten and are satisfied, praise the Lord your God for the good land he has given you. Be careful that you do not forget the Lord your God, failing to observe his commands, his laws and his decrees that I am giving you this day. Otherwise, when you eat and are satisfied, when you build fine houses and settle down, and when your herds and flocks grow large and your silver and gold increase and all you have is multiplied, then your heart will become proud and you will forget the Lord your God, who brought you out of Egypt, out of the land of slavery. He led you through the vast and dreadful desert, that thirsty and waterless land, with its venomous snakes and scorpions. He brought you water out of hard rock. He gave you manna to eat in the desert, something your fathers had never known, to humble and to test you so that in the end it might go well with you. You may say to yourself, "My power and the strength of my hands have produced this wealth for me." But remember the Lord your God, for it is he who gives you the ability to produce wealth, and so confirms his covenant, which he swore to your forefathers as it is today.
	If you ever forget the Lord your God and follow other Gods and worship and bow down to them, I testify against you today that you will surely be destroyed. Like the nations the Lord destroyed for not obeying the Lord your God."

Multiple Versions of the Bible are used to give clear understanding and relative content based on the integrity of the interpretation that conveys the author's intention. The Bible Translations used in this book are varied in the translations from these versions as inspired from the online website Biblos.com: **New International Version (©1984), New Living Translation (©2007), English Standard Version (©2001), New American Standard Bible (©1995), Holman Christian Standard Bible (©2009), International Standard Version (©2012), King James Bible (Cambridge Ed.), GOD'S WORD® Translation (©1995), King James 2000 Bible (©2003) and the American King James Version.**